THE RETURN OF THE MAGNIFICENT NINNY AND OTHER POEMS

For Sashi

THE RETURN OF THE MAGNIFICENT NINNY AND OTHER POEMS

by

RAJ DRONAMRAJU

Post Egoism Media
www.postegoism.net

ISBN: 978-0-578-06029-3

CONTENTS

FORWARD

We are by definition definition. We make sense of reality through words. The meaning we strive for is the meaning expressed not something we only know within us but something we can get out and share with other people.

This takes the form of poetry which can be all about form. It is the narrative of the heart and mind freed from the restraints of a narrative structure.

We are by definition seeking definition. Those everyday references we reach for color in the subject and make it come to life. This coloring in is not just a physical description but also involves a statement on the state of the mind as well.

Raj Dronamraju
May 27th

BIOGRAPHY

Raj Dronamraju notices that people often describe themselves through their work. He has worked for a breast implant manufacturer, a dental implant manufacturer, and a company that manufactures sonar apparatus for submarines. He is the author of a six volume semi-autobiographical series of novels of which the second book *THE ABSENT* is available online. Raj Dronamraju is an American but currently lives in Malaysia and teaches English at a local university.

TOMORROW'S DISTURBANCE

Love is in the ears and eyes and mouth
Can't be pushed out or shouted down
Can't be kept away with the contents of an aerosol can
The perfect conditions are there
The bright future is here

Tomorrow, no one will ask you to turn the noise down
Tomorrow, our lifeflow will drown out everything
And if everyone says loud and clear "With me….Sunshine! Respect! Love!"
Our hearts will become steam rollers running over cowards

And tomorrow evil runs out of places to hide
"Here, take all my money….I don't want it!"
Climbing steps two at a time
The world we are looking out at is under new ownership

THE RETURN OF THE MAGNIFICENT NINNY

I am still where I was
All of history and literature flowing through me
Space and time and a kick in the ass
Still, I've got no money
No respect and no visible means of support
One step away from the soup kitchen line
The scales tip in neither direction
Noble but capitalism makes weasels of us all

I'm still taking it all in
Perspective and perception filed under something I'm good at
Everything else might as well be thrown in the trash
For my own peace of mind, I have given up the fight
I will now do what I want
After I give my day to others in exchange for a paycheck

I pledge to terminate all that weakens and degrades us
I pledge to deviate from that which wears me down
I pledge to plug my ears each time they mention spouses and kids
The sundry and trivial details of living
High school graduation, Monday night football
I pledge to say "please" and "thank you"
And be more critical of those who won't
The counter-culture and the counter-counter-culture
The shallowest underground
Here's what I'm about;
Books and the quiet life
Civility and vinegar
The result, not the chase
No celebration of the human race

You would like me to help raise awareness
Of domestic violence and environmental destruction
But I am inspired by a grilled cheese sandwich
Prepared on the stove not in the microwave
The cheese and the bread are equally cooked
There's nothing worse than melted cheese and the bread is not yet brown
Or toasted bread with a cold, unmelted slice of cheese
Remember to butter the outer side of the slices of bread
To prevent them from sticking to the pan
I'm all about the perfect grilled cheese sandwich

SHE MADE LOVE TO A TRAIN

She made love to a train
Then it moved on to another station
Carrying mail and the sordid histories of its passengers

She enquired of the stationmaster
Only to be given a list of departure times
But not the actual whereabouts of the train

She made love to a train
And then her car was decoupled from the engine
And left on the tracks in the middle of nowhere

She spiraled erratically at higher and higher speeds
Someone's tampered with the brakes
The junction has been warned of her approach

GOD'S GETTING TIRED

Hard to think straight when you're tired
The mind cannot crush and absorb information
It's like undigested meat sitting in the digestive tract
Sluggish in the face of the world's rhapsodies
Watching ants climb the wall in smart formation
Why do I even bother?
Anything I create ends up biting me in the ass eventually
One beautiful and inspiring tale of a young girl's kindness towards others
Versus a million stories of man's inhumanity towards other men

I like a curious and logical mind
Despite the fact it might not recognize me
The careful nurturing of fingertips
Reaching through the soil towards a clearer understanding
Just enough to wet the appetite for knowledge
Feed the mind not the pelvis!
The sex drip thingy, that which propels all living things
Drains away and is diluted into nothingness
"I can no longer feel my loins"
The intellectual conquers the animal
And it's about time

Me god and you god try to use their wills to shape life
Visualizing the world as they want it to be
Using the word "will" instead of "like" or "can"
They have been delegated this task by senior management

Hey now, don't think the car is driverless
Me god and you god just have to look out for yourselves
Because I'm in the mood for doing absolutely nothing at all

THESE ARE THE HANDS

These are the hands
That I hold myself down with
And these are the hands
I beat myself up with

And a young girl named Satan rejects my application
While the deep sea diving academy accepts my application

These are the hands
That I ball into fists
And these are the hands
That shake and cannot hold a pencil

Like an alcoholic surgeon injured in a car accident
Wrung the neck of a dove when I found out peace never came

These are the hands
I feel up life with
And these are the hands
I hold up stop! then I act and then I get away

These are the hands
That never meant malice
I never liked the sound of cracking knuckles

THE GIRL WHOSE PICTURE
IS ON THE SIDE OF THE BOX

Today I will count to three
And today I will push in the lock button on my bedroom door
And today I will thrash around alone looking for objects to break in a fit of
       temper

And the things I cannot get
The frustration of being 16 years old
Will stay with me for a lifetime
And I remember….

The girl whose picture is on the cereal box
Be she gymnast, cheerleader, or housewife
Exists only for the purpose of advertisement

And as I turn her upside down to fill my cereal bowl
I think of a utopia where no one lies
And noble nervous wrecks such as I
Are celebrated and revered

But for now,
I draw a moustache on her face
And I cut out her eyes
On the back, 50 cents off further cereal purchases

THE CURSE OF THE WORD

People who curse indiscriminately
Drop the F bomb at random
Fling cuss words like breathing
Turn me off

Nothing uglier than a woman with a sewer for a mouth
The obscenities pouring out make her small, foul, unattractive

This coarse culture
Reminds me of a cheap, plastic veneer
Covering a tasteless, hollow interior
The oil painting of a bullfighter
Gazing down on shag carpeting

HOMELESS IN MIND AS WELL AS BODY

Half-naked insane transient
Seated on the shoulder of the road
He's clearly enjoying life
Despite the fact there's no one at the other end of his animated conversation

Shirtless but he's not Christ
Just unclaimed and broken
Talking to himself on the shoulder of the road
I find honesty in his public insanity
Spare me from idiots acknowledged as thus
But also spare me from idiots who think they're clever

ARRANGED MARRIAGE

Life in motion
Someone forgot to set the parking brake
And I'm powerless

They are old and gather their offspring around them
The years have helped instill the temperament for slavery in the young
The peace of the blood related autocrat is more fragile than it looks

Someone I left today
Baked me tasty dishes
Washed shirts and pants
Kept a spic and span house

The night in motion
An apartment building's on fire
And I'm powerless

Someone I left today
Was always stepping on my cape
Jerking my head back, cutting off air
I'm still powerless but also incognito
Desire hides like a persecuted refugee

THE REIGN OF THE CLASSICIST IS OVER

Half-embracing the snob and his outmoded ideas
Establishing a clear path from point a to point b
He is a poet and a Satan worshipper
Cannot keeps his hands off his own genitals

I'm the good intent which isn't recognized
The new ideas and attempts to communicate them through a new form
Don't need to staple a newspaper to my chest
For you to get my drift

There is no hero for this immeasurable timeline
Throwing your weight around like a big imbecilic kingpin
A stale mind that cannot be aired out
Wild and crazy and hopping on one leg
I'm going to run around bare ass naked

WHORED OUT

When the day comes
I am no longer mistreated by frumps
And there is no cause and effect-ing
Of my shallow grave of a personality

We will all cheer JoJo the Dog-Faced Boy together
Saturdays in the park with JoJo the Dog-Faced Boy
The kids bite deeply into something dark and sweet

Until then I need money for loaves of bread
And soap to wash my balls
This is the forced everyday prostitution
But with one strict condition left intact....
An aversion to the emotionally repugnant

THE BURDEN OF EXISTENCE
IS NOT THAT HEAVY

The world is a donkey
And we kick it when we want it to move
Load it down with heavy objects

Avocado-shaped
The mule headed officer makes the stubborn doldrums break
We are upset and passionate and that's a good thing

The world is a donkey
And we feed it oats once a day
Each day I rise and give the day my all
There is no greater responsibility than this

DO YOU OWN YOURSELF?

I am generating and re-generating hoping to get rid of the desire for
    ownership
All I bear with me should be easy to transport and light in weight and
    thought
Purchases lead to other purchases
My perceptions should be my prize possession

I have so many neckties
Colors, stripes, dots, original designs
I love to collect neckties
You can never have enough neckties
My head swims
Shopping malls put an invisible gas in their ventilation systems that make
shoppers vulnerable to suggestion
Or at least that's the theory

Who owns the stars and the heavens?
I am planting a flag on my personality
Getting a deed issued on my moral character
I will gather all my hemispheres of mood together
Individuality is not for sale

HOUDINI ESCAPING FROM
AN AWKWARD SITUATION

We were born to fall asleep at deadly sterile parties
And cave in at the first drunken jibe thrown our way
Armed with excuses, I can't seem to make it past the beanbag chair
Later that evening, the apparatus of reason completely shuts down

Whereas a younger man would have tossed off a merry line or two
Called it putting in an appearance then gone home
I am powerless to act in the face of twelve o'clock
There is nothing here I have ever wanted

Eating standing up, cradling contempt in one hand
Paper plate in the other
Boosted by the antics of a fool
A diversion counted on
To help us escape from this illusion of a good time

SALT LAKE

She stood dripping, careless, unavoidable
The flat landscape is all around her trailing off into a suggested horizon
Nothing was learned and she is still untouched
Through storms and civil wars and the construction of buildings with
enough floors that it requires taking two different elevators to reach the top
In a convenience store, she is the furthest thing from my mind
Reaching for foodstuffs that are the furthest thing from nature
It's a long way to the sea but she is self-sufficient
And I am my own ocean with a soul many fathoms deep

THE WRONG HOLE

Cutting corners with a reptilian lover
Particles colliding against one another
Passion is no ordinary exclamation against poverty and injustice

I'm tired of what I see every day
Some people should be born mute
One day, you're going to need my help
When your eight-handed auspicious totem boxes you and makes your eyes
        blind

Marking time with the best I could find
I'm going to milk the cow
With a regularity born of contempt

THE EXPLANATION

Call me too critical
And punish the moon
Set the table for the dogs

Hide behind sunglasses worn indoors
Blasphemy hurled on the behalf of dinner guests

I would not divorce myself from writing and speech
Communication failure
Am I to blame?

Losing my way and saying goodbye
Held aloft drunkenly in a Chinese restaurant

The tongue slaps the bitch
Who refused to be quiet
I hope she takes that insult to the grave

I would not restrain the truth
Behind respect for seniority or position
You don't understand me
I am not to blame

BLACK SKY, DEAD TREES, UNHEALTHY CHILDREN

I celebrate nothing
The opposite of Walt Whitman
Least of all humanity

Pale, coughing, enfeebled limbs
They lie cowering
In the corner of damp, unhealthy rooms

The forests are devoid of vegetation
And devoid of life
There is no need to walk quietly here

Somewhere someone once wrote an explanation for all of this
But now there is only darkness
And death at different speeds

TO CONTROL THE MIND

To put the limping animal out if its misery
Bury the corpse and make new plans
Completely erase everything you know
And start again using a universal fixed point

Star-like, I am navigating an unexplored world
Hands no longer in the pockets of the past
Feel the brail of life's new rhythm
Taste the possibilities which have suddenly appeared

Good health for the mind and body
Stamp out the flames of the self-immolating masochist
Wrestle and subdue the flailing, chaotic world
Will I be able to pin it to the mat until the count of three?

PAVEMENT ARTIST

I came directly from somewhere burned
Somewhere used up, somewhere worn and empty
All that we have is the mind
We write and perform our own television shows
We hoard pencil and paper as if valuable commodities
We make boardgames out of cardboard
And dice out of rocks and animal bone

This umpteenth generation of poverty
Are forced to make their own entertainment
We were given two hands and a brain
And the ability to use them to improvise
Improvise! Our creative ramrods will never be blocked
That's a rich man luxury
We're hungry and salivating to express
Let us seize the tools, brothers and sisters
The next revolution will be left brain vs. right brain

THE FATAL FLAWS OF THE ARCHITECT

The inability to acknowledge failure
An overwhelming arrogance that blots out life itself
The task of creation is overrated
Now there's a godlike pause in the abandoned home of the mind
What are called good qualities are now so corroded they have become a
      cliché

What took minutes to build, it takes years to destroy
And it's not for a lack of trying
The testimony of associates and bottled up emotions
Asking if they could use a blackboard to make it clearer to the panel
Under attack from all sides
The customers won't pay up and the food tasters have all run away

I want to build but lack an artist's sense of the intangible
So I turned to college courses in architecture to prop up my spine
My, what an earnest young man
For the meaty part of the twentieth century

Time froze the soul's rottenness
Cleverness bewitched those who provide building materials and the crew
They said don't let your eyes be bigger than your stomach
But my appetites are large and boundless
In order to feed a lust to add to posterity
The excuse of the artist, the father, the kinky creator, the passionate
      megalomaniac

Boyhood cleared a path
That only fate and will together can elaborate on
Presently, the facts are in the process of razing everything he has ever built
He's left with only a plea that cannot help but touch the hearts of the gallery
"Somebody put me back together again!"

CUP OF CHAMPIONS

On two legs passed by four wheels
The young girl in the backseat makes a face as the car whizzes by
The shoulder of the road is not a safe place to be
Especially when going in the same direction as traffic

Fatalism on two legs
Witness to the constantly unfolding human drama
Product of the sink or swim class structure

And the burglars took everything but the old lady's hearing aid
And at night the park across the street fills with some very strange characters
And I hold all these details inside me
And walk across this land looking for more

And I would never lower myself to drink from the fetid well of self-defeat
Nor would I write a sad letter to produce a formal response from the barest
        of acquaintances

The maid from two houses up the street is hiding in the bushes to make a
        phone call
She takes great care not to be seen
On two legs, I know she is calling a man
Who will approach her on four legs

And the rutting urge is stratospherically below where I am now
Poised for receipt of my trophy
"Thank you to everyone who made this possible"
I shook hands with what was real but it did not let go

FIRST PULL THEN PUSH
THEN RELEASE AND IT'S YOU

Chief among the sideshow freaks is the Indian Rubber Man
With the ability to pull the skin on his cheeks and neck and torso far from
    his body
The laws of human anatomy he was born without regard for
He has stretched his way around and under the tightest social conventions

Tagalong younger brother/stray dog/no longer wanted girlfriend
Grins and bares its teeth
Five minutes after the last kick
They live for holding back their abuser
Content to weld and link their own chains

And which one of the following are you?
Broken and recast in another's self-image or
So wild and free as to be a permanent outcast

So which one of the following are you?
The one that moulds the shape dispassionately, creatively or
The patterned life form with about as much uniqueness as an Arizona tract
home unable to do a single thing differently

NO GOD

Once there was a god
That we made up
To explain fire and babies and lightning and death

Once there was a god
That we used as a weapon
Against types of people we didn't like

Once there was a man
Who was scared of the vastness of the universe
And other natural phenomenon he didn't have the knowledge to explain

Once there was a civilization
That voluntarily put itself in the chains
Of myth and superstition

UPON ABDICATION OF THE THRONE
BY THE QUEEN OF THE MOLE PEOPLE

Oh absence
Which makes the heart not fonder but harder, stiffer, colder
That tells us nothing though we expect enlightenment
At least carrying forward a smile to be used at a future date

The origin of the nickname "Queen of the Mole People"
The result of a joke about the subterranean nature of our temporary
        classroom
Beloved diva, you wore it proudly for the love of friends and peers

One day, we will turn around and realize that we had the time of our lives
And attempt to reclaim the moment, the adventure
That's a journey that defies the natural order
The natural order is change

Because life is about saying goodbye to people you've known and cared
        about
While drudgery pulls us mechanically forwards
We hold on to moments that have no permanence

THE DOWN DOWN TASTE

I've got nothing but hatred for you
Goddamn this planet that spawned you
Goddamn the womb that developed you
Goddamn the existence that holds you upright
Your existence is reason enough not to believe in a God

Thoughts of your suffering are like pleasant daydreams
I fantasize about harming your family with you forced to watch
Tied up with ropes, your tongue is clattering and imbecilic
I wish my benediction of hatred could take on physical form
And you could know its physical form
You cry like a girl as it prepares to do the unspeakable
This massive blackness makes it like you never existed

Outside, Nicole is hanging the laundry
I breathe in deeply, my forehead's warm to the touch
These are the afternoons of reflection and triumph
These are the afternoons that practice self-control
Eyes squinting tightly, no one lets me down easy
The night of a thousand footsteps is approaching
Restless insomnia footsteps

When Nicole shudders and awakes and asks why I'm not sleeping
I cough up an answer half-mumble, half-lie
I'm on the border....rage is on the other side
A Mexican stand-off lasting nearly three decades
I don't expect to ever win this

SHE SANG AT THE POST OFFICE

She sang at the post office
"My grandfather touched me inappropriately"
Resist going berserk to don a mask of studied apathy
Perish boredom, perish religion, perish blue jean mini-skirts

She sang at the post office
"I am the XYZ communicator"
Committed followers are hard to come by
Such grandiose thoughts seem ridiculous

At the flea market, at the garage sale
She sits among the dog eared out of print paperbacks
The lamps without shades, the three-legged chairs
Sprawled on top of grief's kingdom
She must have monotony to cling to

THE IRAQ WAR IN HUMAN TERMS

And when Mrs. Scleroso got the bad news, she dropped the bag of rice she
    was holding
The contents spread out across the kitchen floor
The sound of her slippers crushing the hard grains of rice sounded like the
demonic cackling of small evil beings such as gremlins or gnomes

She had the presence of mind not to drop the phone
Now Mrs. Scleroso called everyone she could think of
And all she could think of were questions

Oh, how could this happen?
Why didn't I make a stand?
How could I just go along to get along?
And how could I not think that your blood, which is also partly my blood,
might end up spilled on a cracked Baghdad street?

It comes to mind not to put your trust in an organization that chews up and
spits out those who volunteer for it
I was a patriot until they confiscated my son
Now I know the red white and blue was a veil restricting my vision
She thinks of her loss and the mourning mothers in other lands
We will weep for our dead children

THE CASTE SYSTEM AGAIN (?)

For I am no one and you are someone
Press a button and wait for a response
For I am nobody and you are everybody
Check your head at the door

A stopped clock is right twice a day
I don't want to save you with a camcorder
I want to imperfectly remember you
How I see you embellished by emotion, distance, perspective
When I meet you sometime later, I can't recognize you

For I am loneliness and you are togetherness
These are the hours that wear away indifference
But I am the prototype and you are the most commonly purchased model
And what comes in between is what we feel

THE REVERSE PROMETHEUS

I'd like to take the fire away
Maybe for a century or two
Let humanity cool off
The trickster of folklore is not I
It's time for truth not mythology
Let's find out if it is possible to put the genie back in its bottle
Before the human race finally succeeds in committing global suicide
Then we can all get back to basic human needs
Make a pact against loneliness
We must endure

But I'm trapped
Sometimes it feels like vultures are chewing on my innards
A thousand Hercules couldn't free me from my bonds

GHOST STORY

The sound of a ghostly piano
Filtering through an empty house
Footsteps of a phantom in this damp, dark house
Who opened the closed door? Who moved the dishes?
Various tenants shudder
They are never comfortable here and move on quickly

Bringer of turmoil, unease, and death
Someone's trying to send me a message
Speak to me now in the soft moan of nightmares
"I wish they knew the child that became the I"
Meet the originator and the progenitor at the same time

O machines of gothic imagery
Dumb with chains of karmic heaviness
They committed a crime against nature
And left behind a physical presence

But we do not scare easy
We are brash attitudes and tight t-shirts
It's easy to write about death
Harder to work up an interest in living

THE WORLD IS FULL OF
THE MENTALLY RETARDED

The world is full of the mentally retarded
He has special needs
We all have needs that are special

But you are high functioning
You have a job....fulfilling society's obligations
They call you normal
But there is no common sense in your brain
Incurious, dull, stupefied
Lacking basic knowledge and skills

I'm not sure what's wrong in customer service
"May I talk to your supervisor?"
Why do you work in customer service?
You don't understand a word I say
Or the basic duties of your job

But you have a job and they say you are normal
I must disagree
Your idiot stare and Down 's Syndrome conversations give you away
But you will marry and have children
Keep the idiot gene going

Your progeny will inherit the Earth
Maybe one of them will invent a cure for Cancer
But I doubt it

THE UNSETTLED MIND

Pudding, you have frustrated me for the last time
And
Pudding, I have committed acts of extraordinary violence four times in my
      life
And
Pudding, check and recheck the presentability of me
And
Pudding, there is a logic and the mind which refuses to accept it
And
Pudding, I wish I could impress upon you the importance of
      communication

She overpowers me in the backyard of reason
Fierce, relentless, strong, won't take yes for an answer
No stopping her until all hope is scoured from the scene

My arm is twisted up into the small of my back
I'm going to shout uncle any second now

I accept the decision
She said "gonads make me cry"
Threatening and distant turn her on
Threatening and distant I am not

SELF-PITY IN A TENT CITY

There are no words to express how I fell out of love with humanity
And in a tent city of faceless souls
There is plenty of time to think back
Past doubt, past pain, there is cardboard and there is desperation
What I had once was not appreciated
So it took flight and scattered
Leaving me alone in unexplored wilderness
And in a tent city of downtrodden anonymity
Hardened emotions are hardly a reward
My accumulated life is fast falling apart

VOICE O'LITERARY

What is poetry?
What is Dronamraju?
I take on the role of the dragon at the gate

Real names are proof of nothing except the desire to mythologize self
"I can hardly stand myself" chants the manic depressive bard

What is feeling?
What happened to the elementary school I attended from second to fifth
        grade?
Time in the narrative is akin to the big stall
Like boxers too tired for further blows hugging one another

We select a mood based on a past experience
And we are conditioned to slip in and out of these moods expertly
"Boo hoo hoo that was 1977"
"Yipppeee that was 1987"

DEAR FRIENDS

Living here is making me ill and unhappy
And desperate to find meaning in life
Oh you setters of agenda
Please add this to next week's timetable

When the curtain falls and we are left alone with our thoughts
We reflect on dear friends who are not with us at the moment
This circling routine which found us aligned
One or both of us is no longer part of

Dear friends who share the same interests
And opinions on the patterns of living
And who found the world obnoxious, unicorn-like
Don't let it poke a hole in your sense of knowing what you have

Oh you setters of agenda
Now I've bottomed out in this place
Oh you setters of agenda
Give me another chance to be grateful for what I have

WHO'S CHASING WHOM?

As you bring down the portcullis
Repelling invaders and allies alike
Do a self-critique of your reverse psychology
Not knowing makes you even more of a tease
I'm writing this in the darkness
Not really caring if you ever read it

I sit in the Emergency Bar at the Suen Hotel
Nursing a gin and tonic
I spy your shadow presence out of the corner of my eye
But don't care
The night manager wiggles his finger bringing down the life of the evening

Hallelujah! I don't want anyone and no one wants me
Hallelujah! I boycott life....Let riot police beat on my extraordinary sense
            of identity with truncheons

I wish life between the two sexes was easier
And those who charge for service were younger and better looking
I grit my teeth in the Suen Hotel....It's like being barbecued.

Come in if you're going to come in
Stay out if you're going to stay out
Hallelujah! Oblivious rapscallions caught with their pants down
Hallelujah! Why did you punch me in the arm?
Soft and feminine so playfully
You must have had brothers at home when you were a child

NO ROOM FOR NOSTALGIA

I hate the good old days
I hate all this talk about the good old days
Ahead are the best days
As we get smarter and fitter and more alert

But let's ignore all that
And talk about the times when we had no money, no friends, and were
        miserable
As if they were glorious

Five years from now, I will be happier than I am now
Five years ago, I wasn't as happy as I am now
Twenty years ago, I wished I was dead
Under no circumstance would I want to revisit or celebrate these times

What I produce and give to others
Is healthier, higher quality
And what I give the world
Is better behavior imbued with hope

CONFESSIONS OF A FAILED DIPLOMAT

I don't know when exactly your hand slipped from mine
Your arm and body no longer clinging to mine
Falling back into the sea
I caught a glimpse of your head slipping beneath the water
Where were you when negotiations broke down?

Now I live off the earnings of an older woman
And tell my story to anyone who will listen
Global postings form the material for a gifted raconteur
Tales from the bargaining table
She said "what do you have to offer?"
And I said "nothing"

Shot off a flare for a rescue party that's not coming
There will be celebrations across this regressing country
Victorious hands tearing down all the posters and banners
While the expelled former leaders hide in basements and the country
The two sides couldn't agree on any of the original points
I broke every truce with the one I love

GARBAGE TRUCK

Fiction is what's behind guilt
And every single story ever told
Keeping your invective to yourself
When they roll their eyes at your perceived lack of authenticity
Cue these sounds; blowing one's nose, moving around restlessly, snoring

Keeping my invective to myself
At 6:30 AM on Mondays and Thursdays
Time to pick up the garbage
Garbage can lids sealed tightly to prevent animals from scattering the
        contents
Two men crushed to death by accident
The garbage compactor emergency switch wasn't working properly
Splat! went the interruption to a human's machine-like focus

UNCREDITED

I am the grain of sand that rubbed the oyster raw
But all the credit for the pearl was given to the oyster not me
The loud ones with their hands in the air
"Me, me, me" they are shouting
They will grab all the praise handed out even though they did nothing

And when they speak in such sly and unctuous tones
Imagining that you really don't know what they say about you
And how they slither in a devolutionary pattern
Ending in the slime at the water's edge

I am the lighthouse keeper that brought the ship to safety
But the lighthouse is listed as a historical monument and I'm but an
        employee
I've only just started to grasp basic dishonesty as a paramount vice/virtue of
        humanity
Hey liar, my silence is your dirty mirror

THE ALTERNATIVE ENTHUSIASM

If I did unto others as they did unto me
(They meaning those with no sense of time or urgency)
And I cooled myself at night with dissolution
There wouldn't be a straightjacket that could hold me

A helix of unpleasant associations that undercuts living at the same angle
      repeatedly
Triggering all kinds of wild foolishness
I don't want to catch this boomerang but feel compelled to
From then on, strange nobodies fill you with gassy compliments
You are so handsome but I don't care
You are extremely intelligent but I don't care
You are articulate and well-spoken but I don't care
No solid value in these unctuous phrases
Instead, drifting into dark moods, prejudices that snap and growl, impatient
      outbursts
I don't lift a finger but demand change
Laziness is the greatest crime of all
Freeing myself, I turn over and go to sleep

WE LOVE LIKE A CAR ACCIDENT

Our fragile bodies
Are easily torn asunder
By collisions of moving vehicles

The ego and the superego
Put into intensive care
By collisions of moving psyches

Headfirst through the windshield
I mourned all through the night
Until the next day's busy rush hour

Bumper to bumper
I am not without feeling
Hate to drive alone after a collision

FRIENDLY HILLSIDE TOWNS

Being served tea in the village of the dream
Improbable dwellings haphazardly on hills that are like bumps on a teenage
      girl's arm
Lately, I've become too serious
Now, as a guest of comfort, I could sink into a thousand year meditation

Contentment found in houses like little boxes
Everyone here comes equipped with a smile and an invitation
Walking the uneven streets of friendly hillside towns
Is a pleasure I look forward to

His beautiful carnivorous mind
Caged by the choices of childhood
There are worse ways to spend a life
Unless you have known the inverse, don't knock peace and security

THE LOVE THAT WAS
UNCONDITIONAL AND FREE

I fall in love at least ten times a day
As an adolescent but more so as an adult
Society has conditioned me not to express this love

I love a number of my female co-workers
Married and unmarried, young and middle-aged
I would so dearly love to take each one in my arms
At the sound of the first "good morning"

I feel love for many women I see
Sexual? Yes but I also want to know all about them
Society has taught me this is wrong

Guarded for good reason
Hold me…. a total stranger
At long last freedom
Tears fall as we reflect on this

MY FRIEND THE GIANT KILLER

My friend with the slingshot has killed his fair share of giants
Restless for new challenges, he spits in the eye of the daily tyrants
Who seek to collapse our lives into a claustrophobic shape

And the kites that fly and the days it doesn't rain
We wish we could escape our lives
But we are as if stricken mute
Our bodies unmoving as if we were paraplegic

My friend has brought down every Goliath that has confronted him
And slapped me on the back afterwards
I tried to take him on as a role model

I've killed my own share of ghosts and other entities that were not really
            there
I know only too well
What it means to tarnish victory with lack of follow through

EITHER YOU ARE A MAN
OR YOU ARE NOT A MAN

No two ways about it
Above suspicion as he jumps out of the airplane
Pops a wheelie, drives at speeds in excess of 150 mph
But he has never supported a sick wife on a clerk's salary
Or shouldered responsibility far larger than his shoulders

It takes a man to quietly stomach a dead-end job
And put off life by not thinking of anything but now
And men who do strange things to their hair and wear expensive cologne
Well, we have earned the right to laugh at them and call them insulting
      names

A man knows how to grit his teeth and not complain
In the interest of family and responsibility
And those men who can drive a truck or fire a gun
Can swagger with all their might down the boulevard
The real hero goes to bed early as he's got a busy day tomorrow

THE DEATH OF MR. UNIVERSE

Old Mr. Steak and Potatoes
Spanning the globe or never leaving the comfort of his living room
The living organisms under his feet
Snap their fingers and say
"Hey, why didn't I think of that?"

Eviction notice posted in full view
Interrupting hot buttered self-love sessions
Mastodon is too big and slow to escape the glacier
The voices of children sing in unison;
"I WANNA BE YOUR ICE AGE"

THE UPS AND DOWNS OF MARRIAGE

You and me and angelic reasoning
That comes from everywhere and nowhere at once
A brief cessation of hostilities
In this most personal of conflicts
Once again, the little caregiver on my shoulder kicked me in the head
And you with a sloppy mouth and toy button eyes
Stock insults you have committed to memory
I'm carrying you around and it's hurting my back
Why don't you get down and walk for awhile?
A golden dawn comes over sparse vegetation
In the wasteland we created together
I wish I could say this wasn't temporary

SATAN PART 2

For the multi-tentacled holder of eternal temptations
For the turquoise sphere that looks better from a distance
For the doll burning quotient and accompanying hysterical laughter
For the doubts about the platypus and the moon landings
For repeated failures to notice the obvious

For the history we never thought we'd see again
For the bank's meaningless security, where did all the money go?
For the dweller in the cave, be he real or imaginary
For those who shock and gouge human flesh and are held up as heroes
For the desire for weaponry we never seem to outgrow

For Pandora's first broadcast that can never be turned off
For the dull and the half-alive who talk only of fantasy
For the parts of mankind's collective creativity that suck and those that don't
For piercing the blister and watching distraction ooze out
For living in a house without any electricity, phone, and Internet

Perish the old order, tectonic plates shift
Like pirates who plunder their own ships and towns
We are a people who need our relaxation
Chock full of ideas, I write none of them down
Hold on to marriages and funerals
And family dinners and sporting events and happy hours
Lest they take away these trivial pleasures
Meanwhile, giant boulders fall from mountains
Crushing reality but leaving behind priority-free leisure

Pitchfork in hand, is he guarding or waiting?
Does he mean to stop you from getting in or stop you from getting out?
Man needs to satisfy weakness
Too weak to handle any pressure, ironing board people commence folding
        in half

www.ingramcontent.com/pod-product-compliance
Lightning Source LLC
Chambersburg PA
CBHW021015090426
42738CB00007B/792